Joshua k

Youth

Alpha Manual

First published 1995
Reprint November 1997

All rights reserved. No part of this manual or any other *Alpha* resource may be reproduced or transmitted in any form or by any means, electronic or mechanical, including photocopying, recording, or any information storage and retrieval system, without permission in writing from the copyright holder or the expressly authorised agent thereof.

Published by HTB Publications with *Alpha* Resources,
Holy Trinity Brompton, Brompton Road, London, SW7 1JA

Illustrated by Kristy Giddy

Printed in the UK by TPS Print, 6 Warren Lane, London SE18 6BW
Telephone: 0181 317 2997

Index

- Who is Jesus? — 2
- Why did Jesus die? — 8
- How can I be sure of my faith? — 12
- Why and how should I read the Bible? — 16
- Why and how do I pray? — 20
- Who is the Holy Spirit? — 26
- What does the Holy Spirit do? — 30
- How can I be filled with the Spirit? — 33
- How can I resist evil? — 37
- How does God guide us? — 44
- Why and how should we tell others? — 50
- Does God heal today? — 53
- What about the church? — 57
- How can I make the most of the rest of my life? — 63

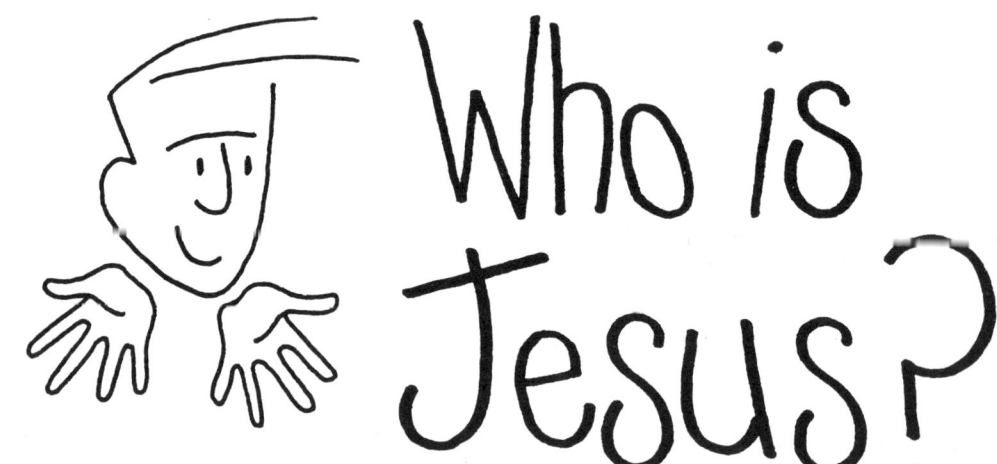

Who is Jesus?

introduction

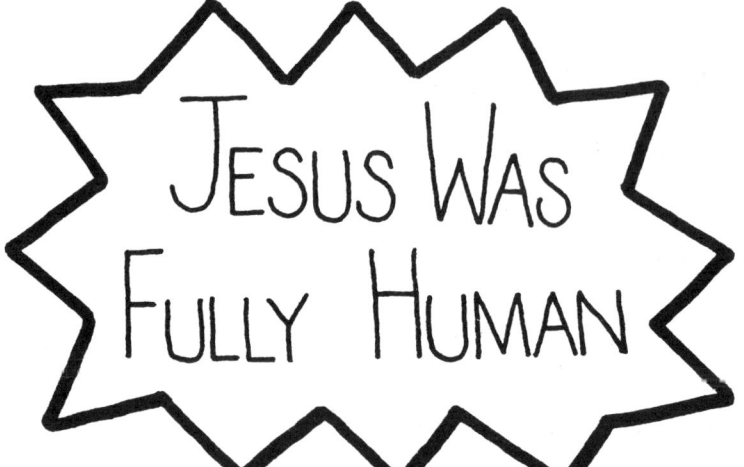

JESUS WAS FULLY HUMAN

✡ He had a human body

that got tired $z Z^Z$ and hungry

✡ He had human emotions

He got angry...   ...and sad

→ MARK 11 vs 15-17   → JOHN 11 vs 32-36

✡ He had human experiences

He was tempted...   He learnt...   and He was obedient

→ MARK 1 v 13   → LUKE 2 vs 46-52   → LUKE 2 vs 51-52

BUT... WAS HE MORE THAN A MAN?

☆ What did He say about Himself?

Jesus said:  I AM...

 ...the Bread of Life  JOHN 6 v 35

 ...the Light of the World  JOHN 8 v 12

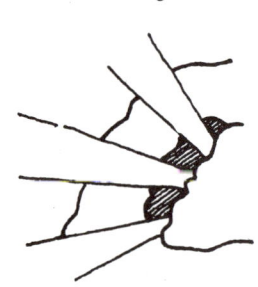 ...the Resurrection and the Life 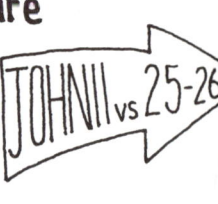 JOHN 11 vs 25-26

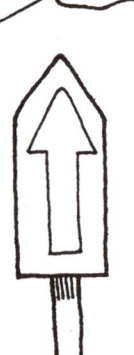 ...the Way, the Truth and the Life  JOHN 14 v 6

☆ Jesus claimed to be:

　☆ The Messiah

　☆ The Son of God

'Either this man was and is the Son of God, or else a madman, or something worse'
(C.S. Lewis)

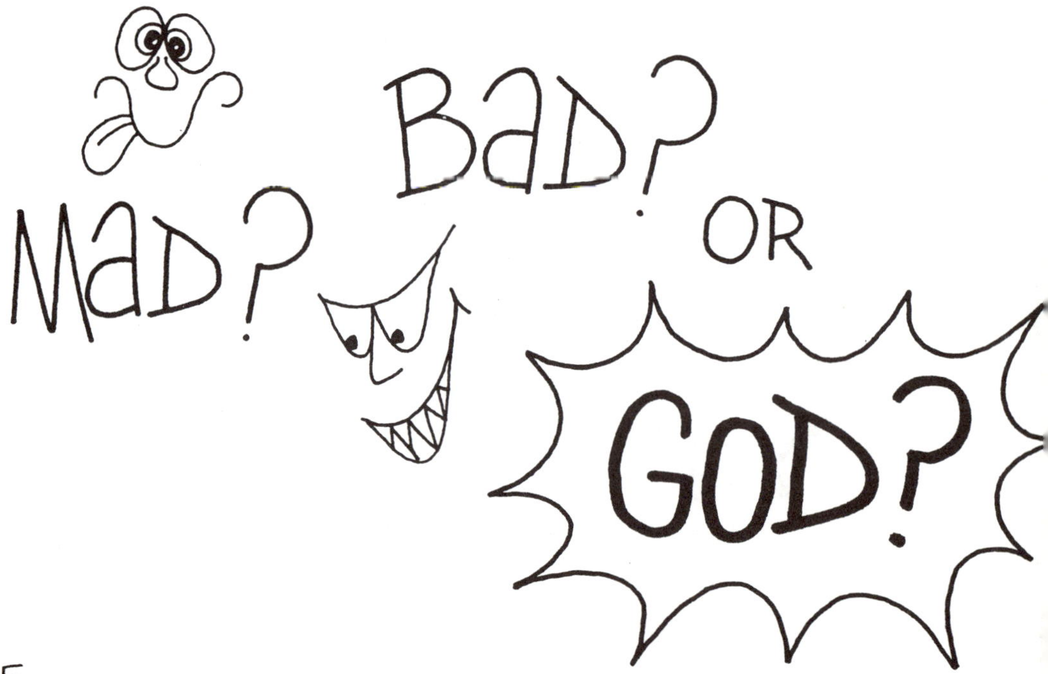

MAD? BAD? OR GOD?

✡ The Evidence:

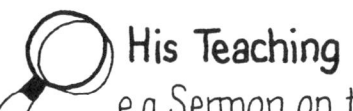 **His Teaching**
e.g. Sermon on the Mount
 MATTHEW 5, 6 + 7

 **His Deeds**
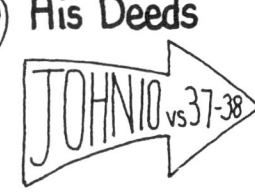 JOHN 10 vs 37-38

 **His Character**

 **His Fulfilment of Old Testament Prophecy**
 LUKE 24 v 44

 **His Power Over Death**
JOHN 11 vs 43-44
 JOHN 21 v 14

✡ The Evidence for Jesus' Resurrection

 **His empty tomb**

Possible Explanations:
1. Jesus didn't die
2. His disciples stole the body
3. The authorities stole the body

 JOHN 19 v 34
MATT 27 vs 62-66

6

🔍 **His appearance to the disciples**

Possible Explanation:
1. They were seeing things
2. He was a ghost

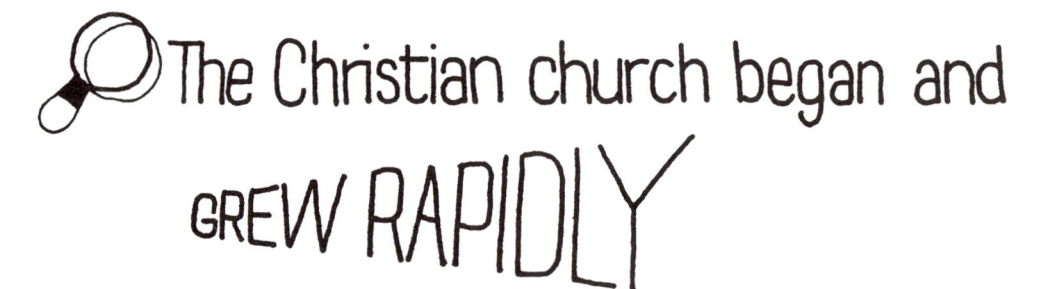

LUKE 24 vs 37-43 →

FAX: 550+ people saw Jesus on 11 different occasions over a period of six weeks

🔍 **The Christian church began and GREW RAPIDLY**

🔍 **2000 years later nearly a third of the world's population know Jesus as their friend and Lord!**

'however strange it may seem, I have to accept the view that He was and is Go[d]
(C.S. Lewis)

Why Did Jesus Die?

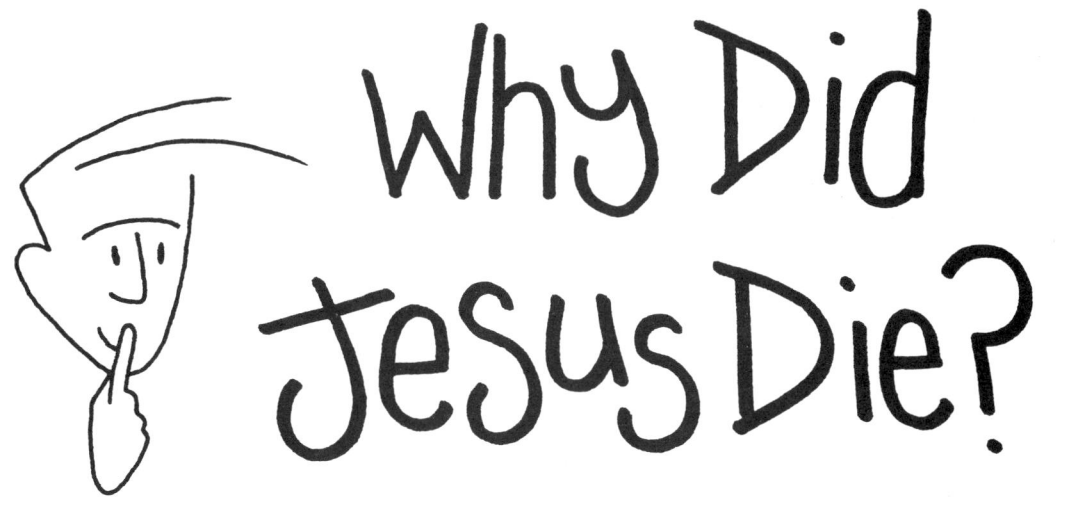

the cross is at the (heart) of the Christian faith

1 CORINTHIANS 2 v 2
1 CORINTHIANS 1 vs 23-24

✡ Mankind's Greatest Need

all have sinned and fall short of the glory of God...

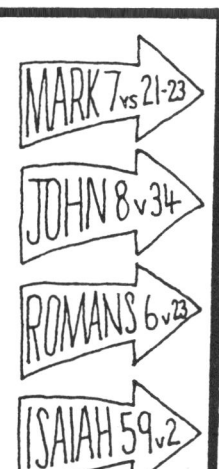

ROMANS 3 v 23

Pollution
Power
Penalty
Partition

MARK 7 vs 21-23
JOHN 8 v 34
ROMANS 6 v 23
ISAIAH 59 v 2

8

☆ What God has done:

Jesus became a substitute for us – He suffered the agony of the cross in our place

1 PETER 2 v. 24

FAX — Crucifixion was the cruellest form of Roman execution. Jesus was flogged with strips of leather interwoven with sharp jagged bone and lead. In front of a jeering crowd He had a crown of thorns pushed onto His head. He was mocked and beaten by a battalion of 600 soldiers, then forced to carry a heavy cross bar until He collapsed.

FAX — At the crucifixion site He was stripped naked and laid on the cross. Six-inch nails were driven into His wrists. His knees were twisted sideways so that His ankles could be nailed. The cross was lifted up and dropped into a socket in the ground. There Jesus hung in intense heat, terrible thirst and unthinkable pain for six hours while His life slowly drained away.

☆ What the Cross achieved:

ROMANS 3 vs 21-26

there are 4 images which can illustrate what Jesus has done for us:

9

1. The Law Court

we are **'justified freely by His grace'** v24

Penalty of sin **Paid!**

Two friends went to school together and became close. As time went by, they both went their separate ways, one to become a judge, the other ending up a criminal. One day the criminal appeared before the judge. The judge recognised his friend and faced a dilemma: his friend had admitted his guilt and the law demanded his punishment, but the judge loved him — he was his friend...

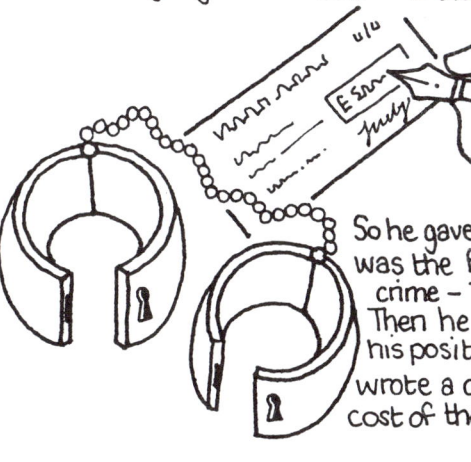

So he gave his friend a fine that was the fair amount for his crime — That was JUSTICE. Then he came down from his position as judge and wrote a cheque to cover the cost of the fine — This is LOVE.

FAX

At the time the Bible was written, someone who had serious debts might well have been forced to sell himself as a slave. Imagine how he would have felt if someone approached him in the market place and on asking how much he owed, paid his debt, and set him free.

'If the Son sets you free, you will be free indeed.' (John 8v36)

2. The Market Place

'the redemption that comes through Jesus Christ' v24

Power of sin **Broken!**

3. The Temple

'God presented Him (Jesus) as a sacrifice' v25

Pollution of sin Removed!

FAX — To deal with sins in the Old Testament a sinner would take an animal that was as near perfect as possible, lay his hands upon it and confess his sins. His sins were passed onto the animal which was then killed as a sacrifice (or substitute) for his sins.

4. The Home

Reconciliation

'God was in Christ making peace between the world and himself' (v.)

2 CORINTHIANS 5 v 19

Jesus died so that we can be put right with God

ISAIAH 53 v 6

'the Lord has put on Him the punishment for all the evil we have done' (v.)

FAX — If you had been the only person in the world, Jesus would have died for you

GALATIANS 2 v 20

How Can I Be Sure Of My Faith?

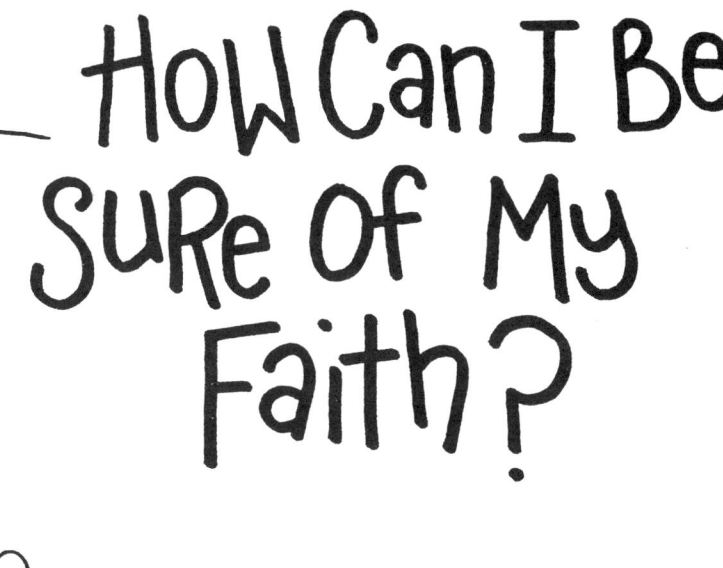

'When someone becomes a Christian he becomes a brand new person inside. He is not the same anymore. A new life has begun' (L.B)

2 CORINTHIANS 5 v 17

BUT: everyone is different — some notice changes straight away — for others it is more gradual — **GOD WANTS US TO BE SURE**

When we **believe in Jesus** we become **a child of God**

JOHN 1 v 12

1 JOHN 5 v 13

☆ The Word of God

Instead of trusting in our own feelings which can fool us, we should trust God's promises from:

Faith = taking God's promises and daring to believe them!

☆ 'I will come in'

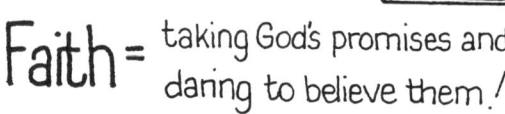
REVELATION 3 v 20

☆ 'I am with you always'

MATTHEW 28 v 20

☆ 'I give them eternal life'

JOHN 10 v 28

13

☆ The Work of Jesus

The things we do wrong – sins – cause a barrier between us and God which can prevent us from knowing His love and make Him seem far away. Jesus never did anything wrong – never sinned – and there was no barrier between Him and His Father. On the cross, God transferred our sins onto Jesus. When He cried out 'My God, my God, why have you forsaken me?' (Mark 15 v 34) Jesus was cut off totally from God, His Father – not because of His sins, but because of ours.

we can never earn God's forgiveness: Jesus died to destroy the barrier between us and God!

☆ God loves us and Jesus died to prove it JOHN 3 v 16 ▷

☆ He took our sins upon Himself

ISAIAH 53 v 6 ▷   1 PETER 2 v 24 ▷

14

The Witness of the Spirit

When someone becomes a Christian, God's Holy Spirit comes to live within them

ROMANS 8 v9

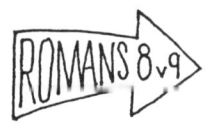

He changes us on the inside:

1. Our character

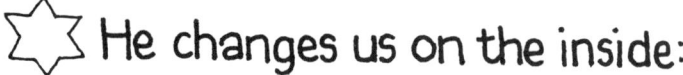

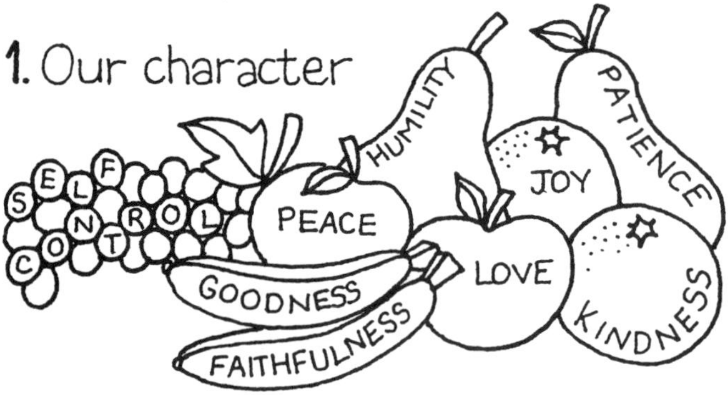

GALATIANS 5 vs 22-23

This passage calls the good things that the Holy Spirit produces in our lives 'the fruit of the Spirit'.

2. Our relationships

With the Holy Spirit at work in our lives – things change! Have you noticed any of these changes?
Look again in a few weeks...

	not much	a bit	loads
a new love for God			
a desire to read the Bible			
a new sense of forgiveness			
a new concern for others			
enjoying worshipping God			
a desire to meet with other Christians			

He makes us sure we are God's child

ROMANS 8 vs 15-16

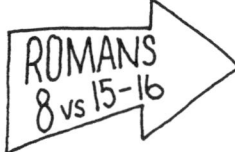

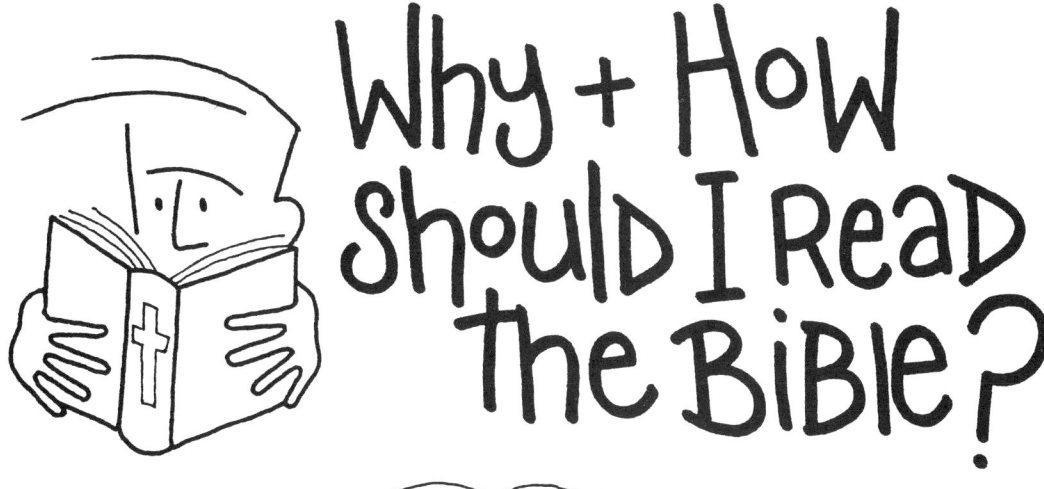

Why + How Should I Read the Bible?

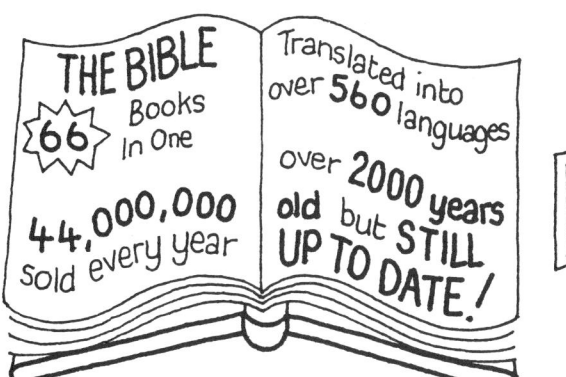

THE BIBLE
66 Books In One
44,000,000 sold every year
Translated into over 560 languages
over 2000 years old but STILL UP TO DATE!

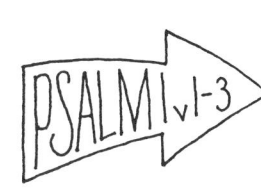

PSALM 1 v1-3

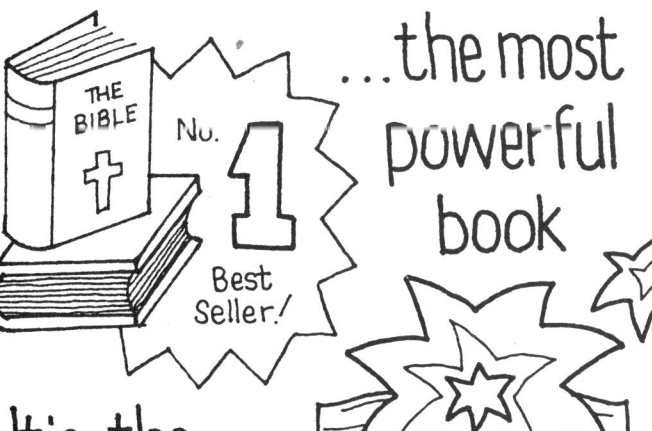

THE BIBLE
No. 1
Best Seller!

...the most powerful book

THE BIBLE

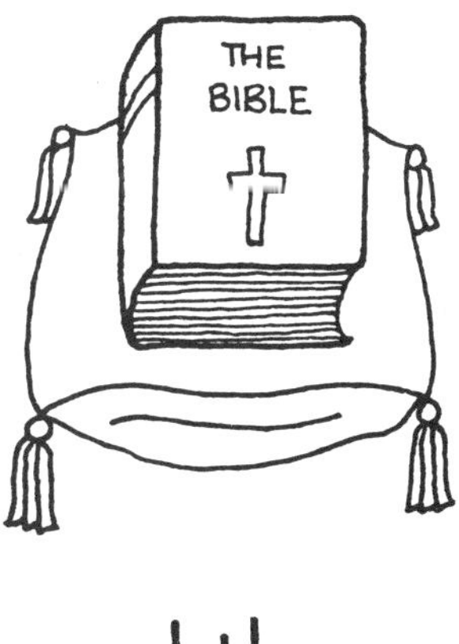

It's the most popular book...

...and the most precious book

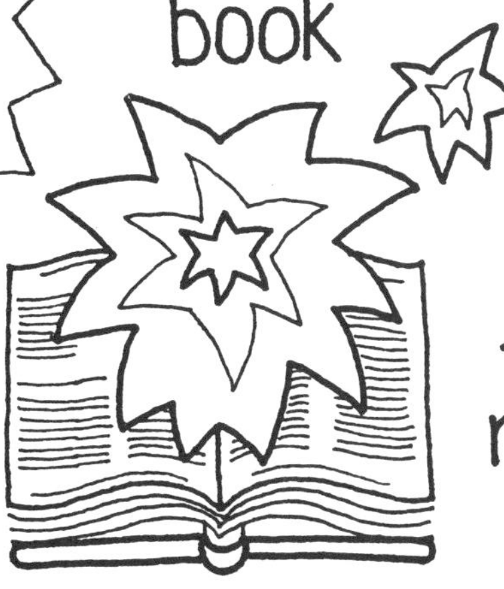

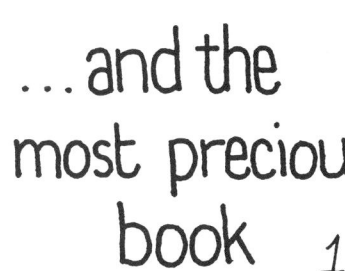

☆ God has spoken

Impress your English teacher with this extremely LONG word:

theopneustos

2 TIMOTHY 3 vs 15-17

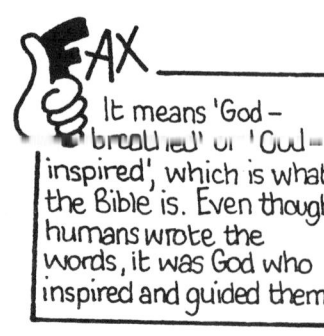

FAX — It means 'God-breathed' or 'God-inspired', which is what the Bible is. Even though humans wrote the words, it was God who inspired and guided them.

We can use the Bible for:

TEACHING · PUTTING PEOPLE RIGHT ABOUT GOD · CORRECTION · TRAINING US HOW TO LIVE FOR GOD

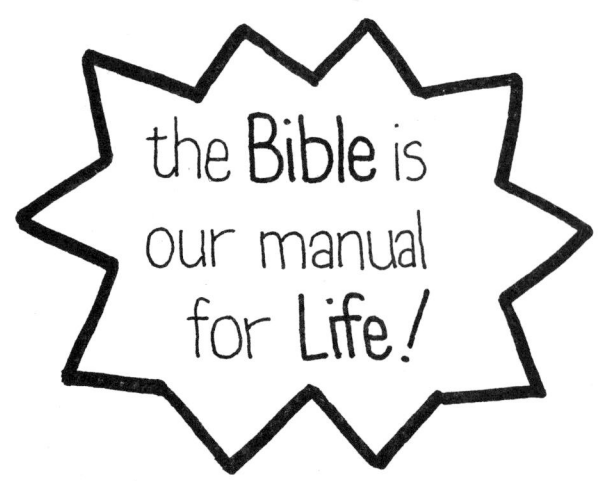

the Bible is our manual for Life!

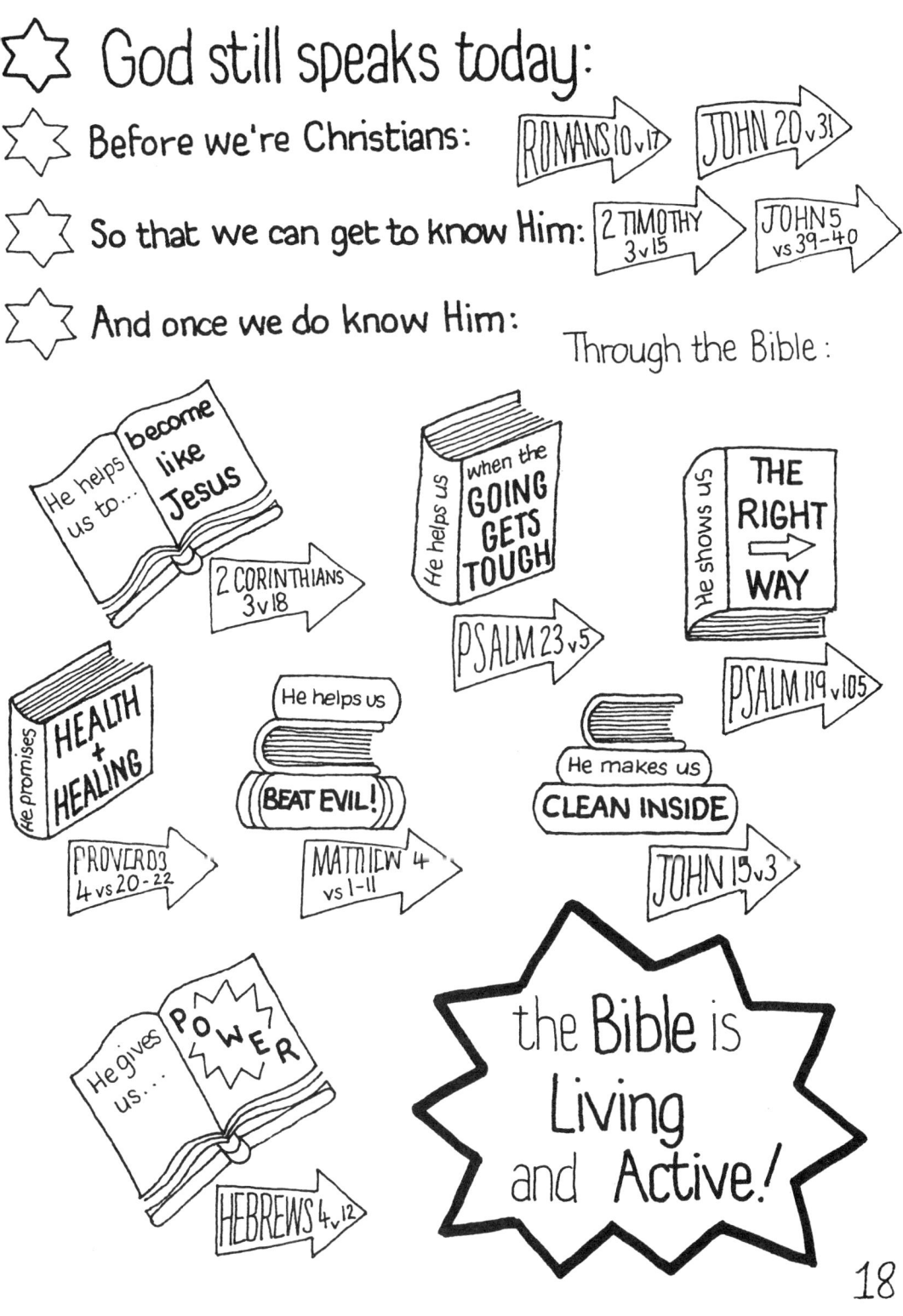

✡ How do we hear God speak through the Bible?

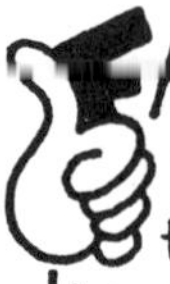

FAX — It's good – but tough! – to get into a routine for reading the Bible. Here's a few tips...

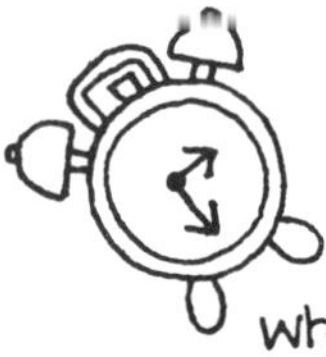

choose a time when you are not rushed or stressed – if you can, it's good to have a regular time

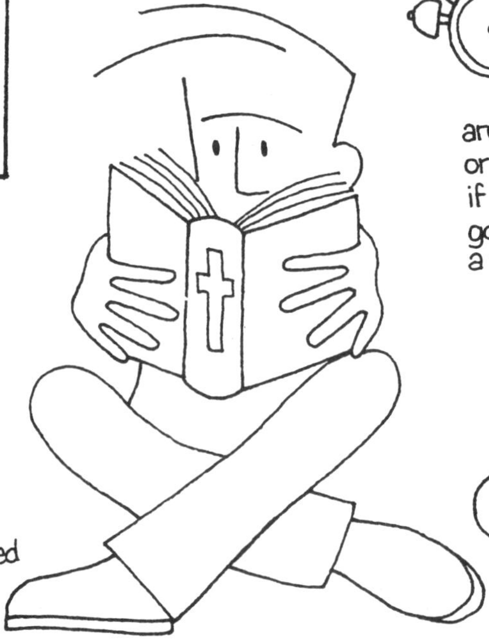

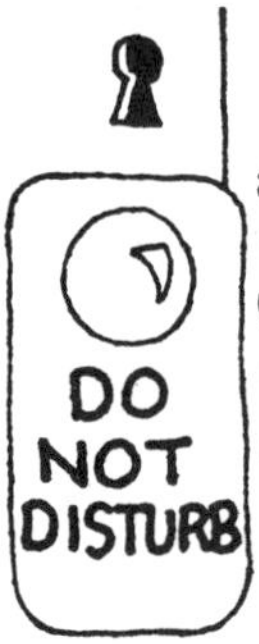

choose a place where you can relax – and where you won't be disturbed

DO NOT DISTURB

MARK 1 v 35 →

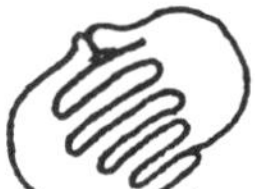

begin by praying: ask God to speak to you through what you read.

❗ as you read – DON'T JUST SWITCH OFF! Ask yourself: What does it say? What does it mean? What's it mean to me?

then, put what you've read into practice!

Read it, Learn from it, but most of all – Enjoy it!

19

Why + How Do I Pray?

Praying is the MOST IMPORTANT thing we can do

It's like having a **'Hot-Line'** to **God** – where you can pick up the 'phone and speak to Him at **any time** and in **any place** !

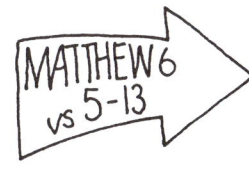

MATTHEW 6 vs 5-13

 We pray:

 To the Father

God's Closeness
'pray to your Father'  MATTHEW 6 v 8

God's Holiness
'Our Father in Heaven' v9

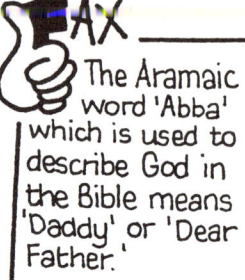
FAX — The Aramaic word 'Abba' which is used to describe God in the Bible means 'Daddy' or 'Dear Father.'

Through the Son

 EPHESIANS 2 v 18

FAX — At the name of **JESUS** every knee shall bow! (Phillipians 2 v 10) (L.B)

In the Spirit

ROMANS 8 v 26

FAX — The Holy Spirit helps us to pray

God the Father
God the Son
God the Holy Spirit

THE TRINITY — FATHER, SON, HOLY SPIRIT

Why Pray?

☆ We build a relationship with God
God loves to hear us and talk to us

FAX — Just like we need to talk to our mates in order to build up a relationship — so we need to talk to God in prayer

☆ We follow Jesus' example
MARK 1 v 35 LUKE 6 vs 12 + 28 LUKE 11 v 1

☆ Rewards of Prayer:
Joy — JOHN 16 v 24   Peace — PHILIPPIANS 4 vs 6-7   MATTHEW 6 v 6

☆ Results of Prayer:
MATTHEW 7 vs 7-11

Ask and you will receive

Seek and you will find

Knock and the door will be opened to you

 Does God Always Answer?

 Things can get in the way...

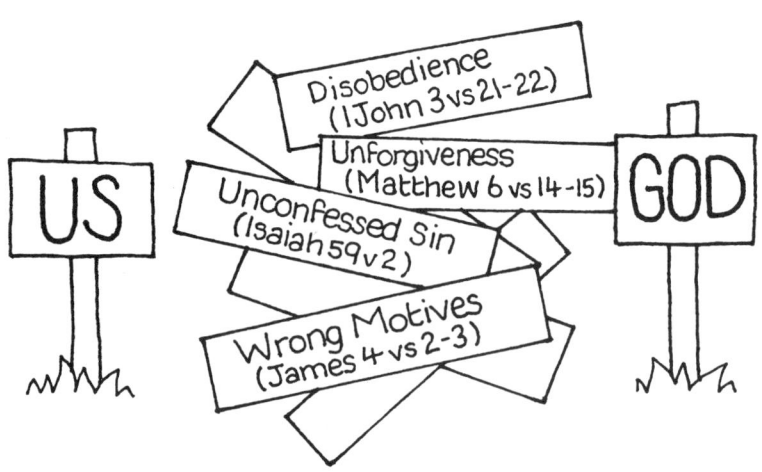

Sometimes we want things that are different from what God wants for us...

All good gifts come from God

MATTHEW 7 v 11

Sometimes God says no – because it's not good for us or others

GOD ALWAYS WANTS THE BEST FOR US!

☆ How Do We Pray?

Thankyou: Praising God for who He is and what He's given us

Sorry: Admitting where we've gone wrong and asking God's forgiveness

Please: Praying for our own needs and for others etc.

☆ The Lord's Prayer   (OUR FATHER...)

Jesus' example of how to pray:

- 'Hallowed (or Holy) be your name'
- 'Your kingdom come' God's rule in our lives — in the future and now
- 'Your will be done'
- 'Give us this day our daily bread' Both our physical needs and our spiritual needs.
- 'Forgive us our sins as we forgive those who sin against us'
- 'Lead us not into temptation but deliver us from the evil one'

☆ In the New Testament

☆ Beginning with the birth of Jesus

During this time God the Father sent the Holy Spirit in lots of ways:

- JOHN THE BAPTIST LUKE 1 v 15
- MARY LUKE 1 v 35
- ELIZABETH LUKE 1 v 41
- SIMEON LUKE 2 vs 25-27
- ZACHARIAH LUKE 1 v 67

☆ The Holy Spirit was with Jesus right from the start

When Jesus grew up, God His Father gave Him power through the Holy Spirit

LUKE 3 v 22

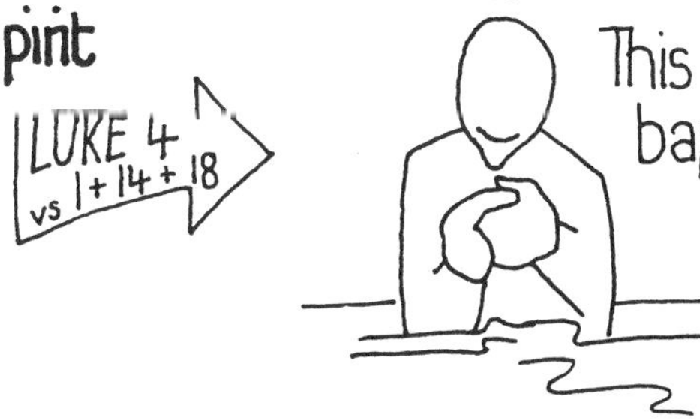

LUKE 4 vs 1 + 14 + 18

This was His baptism

 Gods people were still waiting when...

Jesus announced that soon **everybody** who believed in Him would receive the **Holy Spirit!**

28

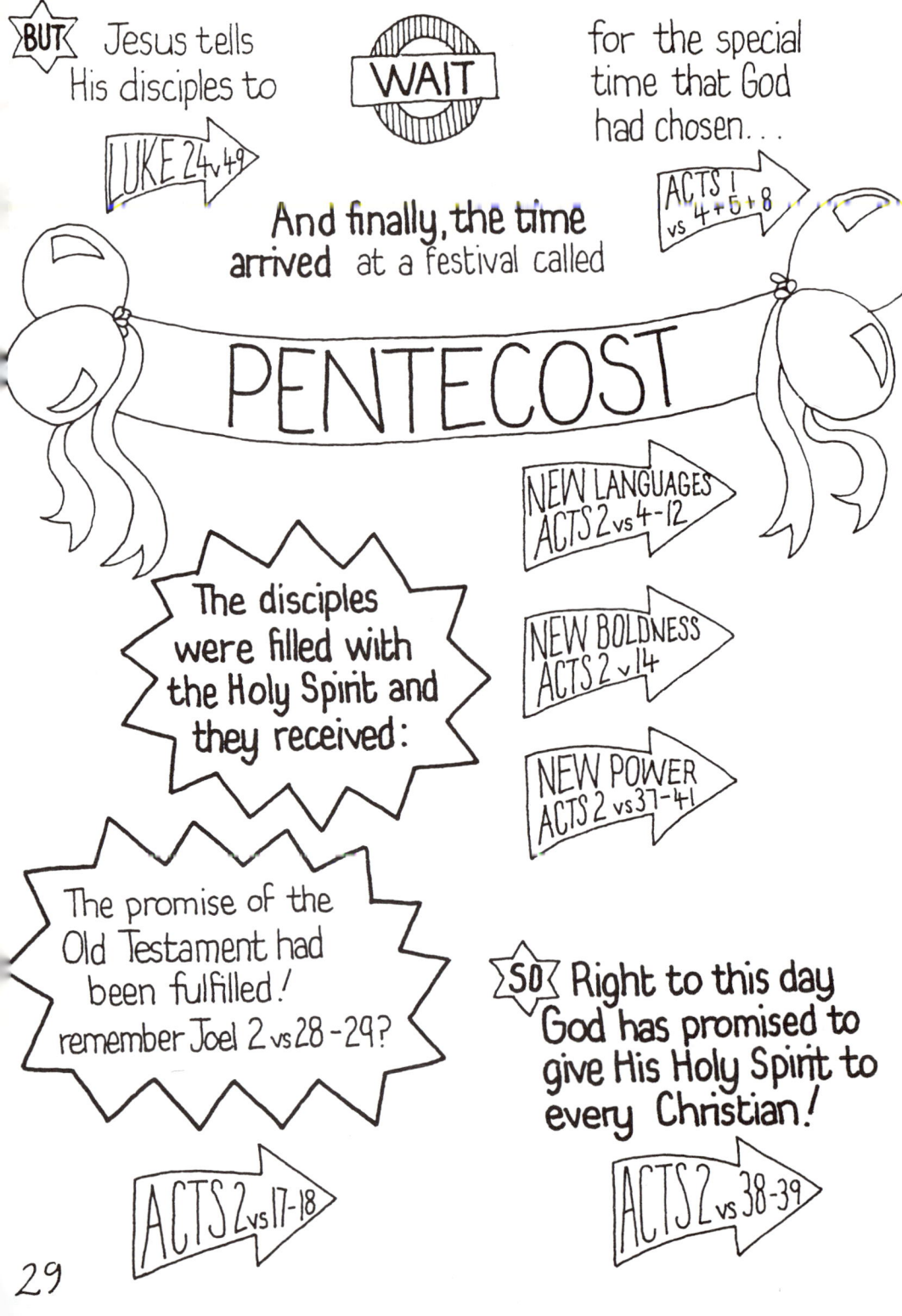

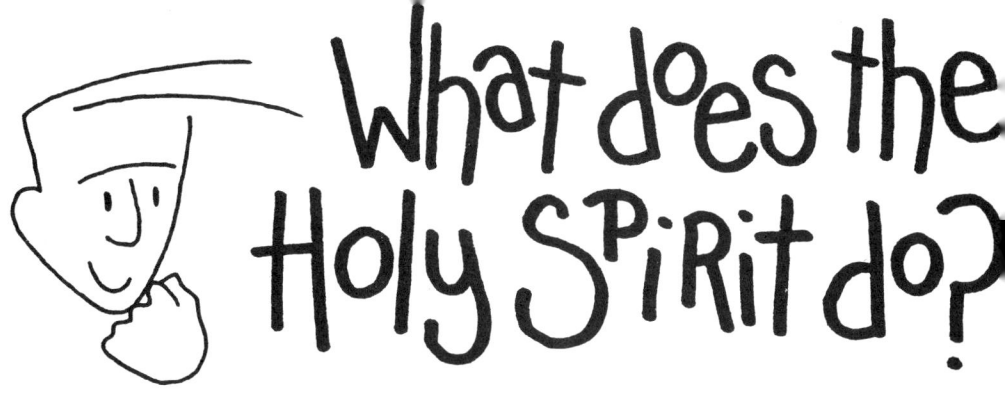
What does the Holy Spirit do?

JOHN 3 vs 5-7

FAX — Just like we are physically born into a human family — so the Holy Spirit gives us a new birth into GOD'S FAMILY!

HE MAKES US: sons and daughters of God

⭐ we have forgiveness  ROMANS 8 vs 1-2

⭐ we become God's children  ROMANS 8 vs 14-16

30

HE GIVES: to all God's children

⭐ every member of the family is different  **I CORINTHIANS 12 vs 1-11**

⭐ free gifts ⭐ for each child ⭐ for everyone's good

HE HELPS: God's family to grow

⭐ He gives us the power to live for Jesus — **ACTS 1 v 8**

⭐ and the courage to tell others

SO Every Christian has the Holy Spirit — **ROMANS 8 v 9**

BUT Not every Christian is filled with the Holy Spirit

The Bible says:

 **EPHESIANS 5 vs 18-20** — **BE FILLED WITH THE SPIRIT**

 **FAX** — It's O.K. to ask God for the desire to be filled with His Holy Spirit again and again and again and ...

How can I be filled with the Spirit?

☆ What happens when people experience the Holy Spirit in their lives?

Look at Acts:

at **Pentecost** when the Holy Spirit filled the disciples for the first time, they felt a 'violent wind' from heaven and tongues of fire rested on each of them. — ACTS 2 vs 2-4

the Holy Spirit came with such power to the Christians in **Samaria** the local magician tried to buy Him! — ACTS 8 vs 14-19

when **Paul** received the Holy Spirit, he could see. — ACTS 9 vs 17-19

the people of **Ephesus** were able to speak God's messages in a new way through the Holy Spirit. — ACTS 19 vs 1-6

When Cornelius and co. received the Holy Spirit:

☆ Everyone knew it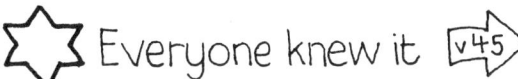

☆ They were released in praise for God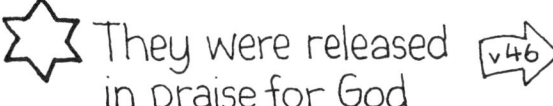

☆ They were given a new language of praise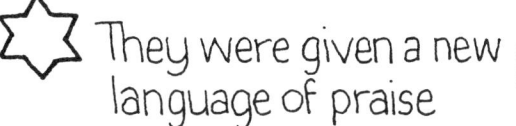

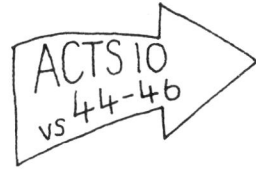

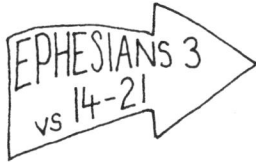

☆ What is the gift of tongues?

☆ It is a **language for prayer** given to us by the Holy Spirit to use whenever we want [v2]

Even though usually we do not understand what we are saying [v14] we can use the gift of tongues to:

pray for ourselves [v4]

pray for others

praise and worship God

Paul says:

- I would like every one of you to speak in tongues [v5]
- don't give messages in tongues in church unless they can be interpreted [v28]
- do not forbid speaking in tongues [v39]

☆ How do we get it?

EAGERLY DESIRE [v1]

☆ **Ask** God to fill you with the Holy Spirit

☆ **Co-operate** - open your mouth!

☆ **Believe** God has good gifts for you - **Persevere**

35

What stops us being filled with the Spirit?

it's all there in **LUKE 11 vs 9-13**

ASK   **SEEK**   **KNOCK**

but there are 3 main barriers:

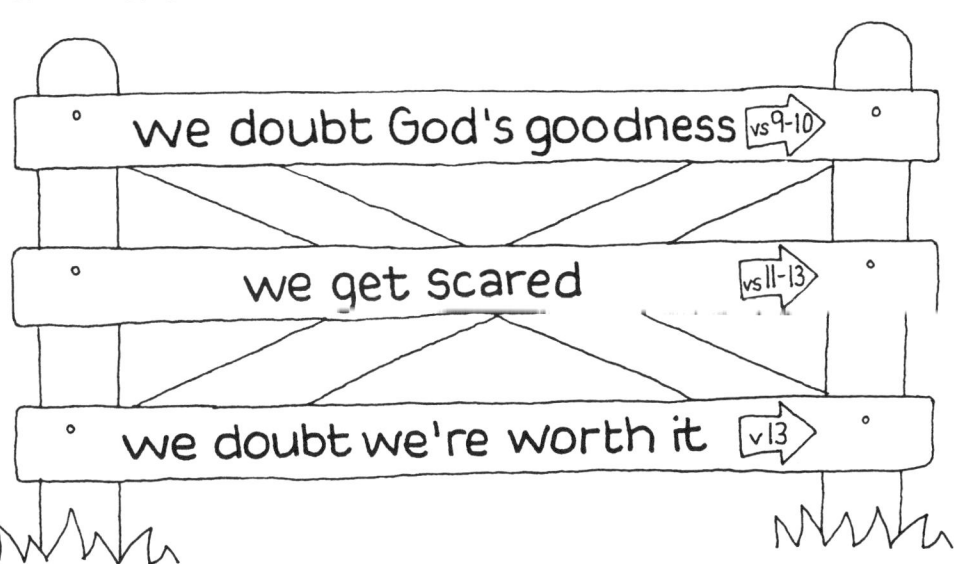

- we doubt God's goodness [vs 9-10]
- we get scared [vs 11-13]
- we doubt we're worth it [v 13]

How Can I Resist evil?

FAX — Have you ever noticed that only one letter separates God from good and evil from the devil

Often our image of the devil is of a red monster with horns and a forked tail

That's pretty different from what the Bible says:

ISAIAH 14 vs 12-21 — In this passage he is called 'morning star' - a beautiful name, but he went bad when he rebelled against God and fell from heaven

The 'king of Babylon' (v.4) is a name for the devil

DON'T get too interested in the devil

BEWARE

DEUTERONOMY 18 vs 10-11

Avoid the things that can lead to an unhealthy interest in the devil. Things like: horoscopes, ouija boards, fortune telling, tarot cards, hypnotism, palm reading etc.

37 GET INTERESTED IN GOD!

✡ In the New Testament we are told that the devil is not just some evil force but that he is **a personal being leading others like him in rebelling against God**.

⚠️ Don't underestimate the devil. He is powerful, cunning and evil.

→ 1 PETER 5 vs 8-11

→ EPHESIANS 6 vs 11-12

FAX — Another name for the devil is Satan. It means enemy — he is Gods enemy and our enemy.

Satan is called **'the father of lies'**

→ JOHN 8 v 44

✡ He is equally pleased when we are tricked into believing either that he is as powerful as God, or that He does not exist at all.

and even happier when we blame God for the state of the world.

✡ If God made the world and everything in it, If He loves us enough to die for each one of us, If He is good and perfect — **why would He mess it all up?**

HE WOULDN'T! that's down to someone else...

38

✡ What are the devil's tactics?

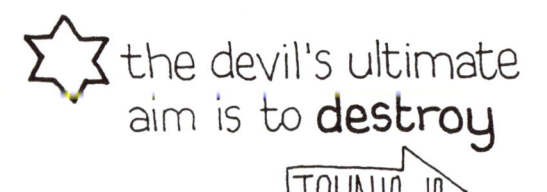

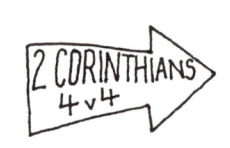

✡ the devil's ultimate aim is to **destroy**

JOHN 10 v 10 ▶

The thief comes only in order to steal, kill and destroy. I have come in order that you might have life - life in all its fullness

✡ he **blinds people's eyes**: stopping them from seeing the Good News about Jesus

2 CORINTHIANS 4 v 4 ▶

✡ he **feeds our minds with doubts**

◀ GENESIS 3 v 1

- does God really love me?
- am I a real Christian?
- why doesn't God hear my prayers

MATTHEW 4 vs 3 + 6 ▶

✡ he **accuses** and **points the finger**:

At God: blaming Him for everything, saying we can't trust Him

At Us: trying to convince us we are failures and that God won't go on forgiving us. He highlights the things we can't do, making us forget the good stuff we can do.

☆ he puts **temptation** in our way — then says 'go on, go a bit further, do it again' until we become addicted to sin.

Look at Adam and Eve:

GENESIS 3 >

God had given Adam and Eve permission to eat the fruit from any tree in the garden but one (vs. 2+3). The devil in the form of the serpent lied to Eve, saying it was really O.K. to do what God had forbidden (vs. 4+5). Eve gave in to temptation and Adam shared the fruit (v. 6). The devil tells us that it is O.K. to sin — he lies — Adam and Eve faced the penalty of their wrongdoing.

☆ They felt embarrassed v.7 >

☆ They hid v.8 >

☆ They were afraid v.10 >

☆ They blamed each other v.12 >

☆ Their friendship with God was broken and they were punished v.14 >

so, do we need to be afraid?

NO! JESUS HAS THE VICTORY

WHERE DO WE STAND?

FAX: Satan is DEFEATED! — COLOSSIANS 2 v 15

FAX: Jesus has AUTHORITY and we have been given authority in His name. — LUKE 10 vs 17-20

COLOSSIANS 1 v 13

Against Satan	⇨ JESUS HAS WON!
Instead of sin	⇨ JESUS FORGIVES
Not slaves to sin	⇨ BUT CHILDREN OF GOD
Instead of death	⇨ JESUS GIVES US LIFE
Instead of destruction	⇨ JESUS IS OUR SALVATION!

Who is the Holy Spirit?

THE TRINITY
FATHER — SON — HOLY SPIRIT

God the Father
God the Son
God the Holy Spirit

The Holy Spirit is talked about throughout the Bible...

✡ In the Old Testament

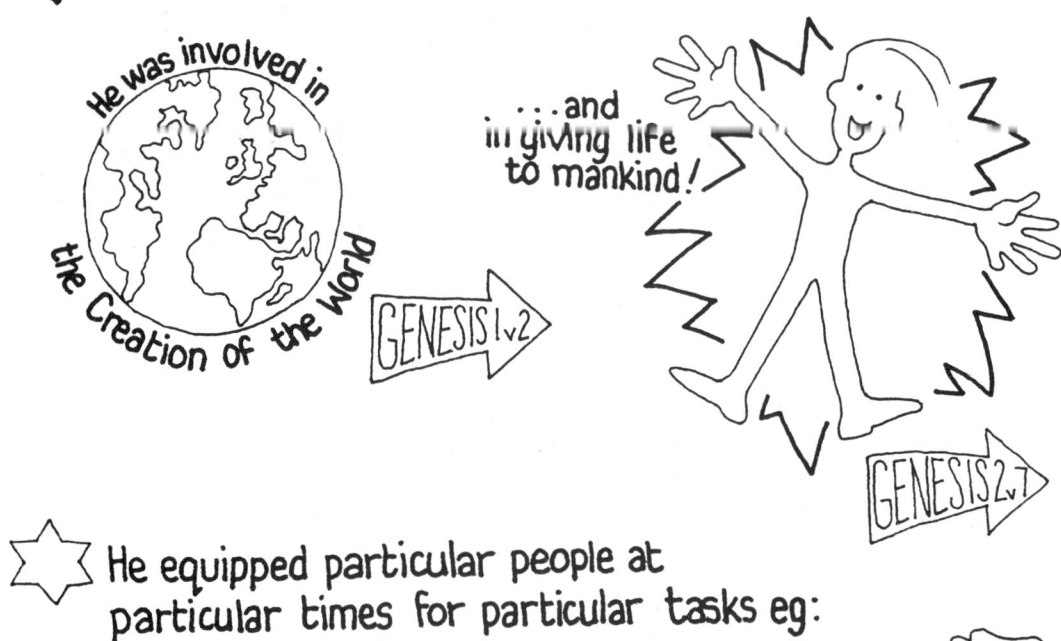

He was involved in the Creation of the World
GENESIS 1 v.2 →

...and in giving life to mankind!
GENESIS 2.7 →

✡ He equipped particular people at particular times for particular tasks eg:

Bezalel — for artistic work
EXODUS 31 vs 1-5 →

Gideon — to be a leader when he felt weak and no good
JUDGES 6 vs 14-16 + v 34 →

Samson — for super strength
JUDGES 15 vs 14-15 →

✡ BUT God promised that the Holy Spirit would come to us in a new way...
JOEL 2 vs 28-29 →

WAIT So God's people waited...

✡ How do we defend ourselves?

EPHESIANS 6 vs 11-18

Breastplate of Righteousness
to protect our hearts from guilt so we know we are right with God
(Philippians 3 v 9)
v14

Helmet of Salvation
to protect our minds from doubt and accusation
v17

Sword of the Spirit
the word of God - the Bible
(Hebrews 4 v 12)
v17

Shield of Faith
makes us sure of Gods promises
v16

Belt of Truth
knowing Jesus' truth to counter Satan's lies
(John 8 v 32)
v14

Boots of the Gospel of Peace
being ready to speak about Jesus
Isaiah 52 vs 7-10
v15

Put on the full armour of God so that you may take your stand against the devil's schemes
v11

☆ How do we attack?

☆ By Praying →2 CORINTHIANS 10v4

the devil trembles when we **PRAY!**

☆ By Action →LUKE 7 v 22

by doing the things Jesus told us to do: spreading the Good News, healing the sick etc.

by His death on the cross **JESUS HAS DEFEATED SATAN FOR GOOD!**

How does God guide us?

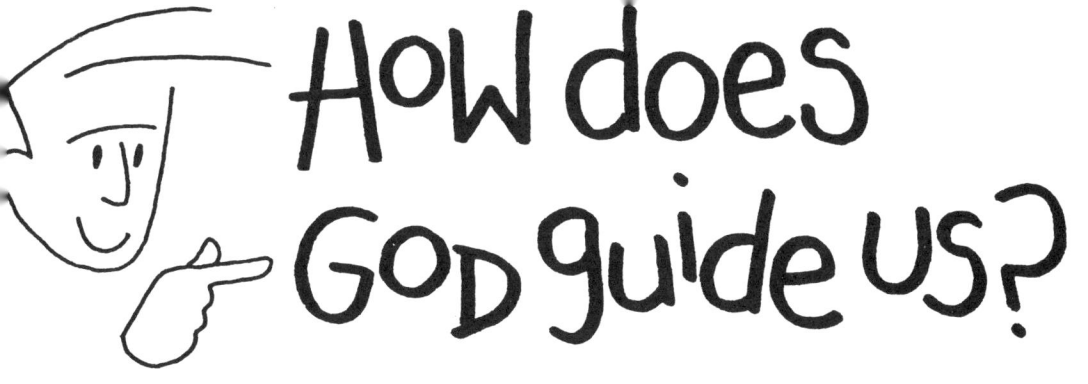

☆ We all have to make decisions:

- WHICH EXAMS TO TAKE
- WHAT TO DO IN THE FUTURE
- WHOM TO ROMANCE AND WHOM TO MARRY
- HOW TO SPEND YOUR MONEY

☆ God promises to guide us when we ask:

PSALM 32 v 8

He calls his own sheep by name... his sheep follow him because they know his voice

JOHN 10 vs 3-4

✡ God has a good plan for each of us

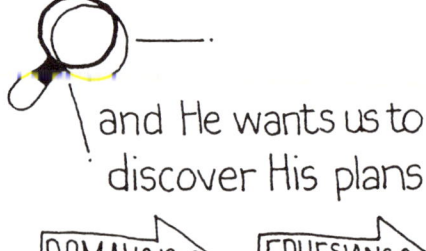

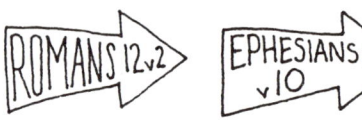

'I have good plans for you, not plans to hurt you. I will give you hope and a good future'

JEREMIAH 29 v11 (YB)

and He wants us to discover His plans

ROMANS 12 v2   EPHESIANS 2 v10

✡ We should talk to God about all our big decisions

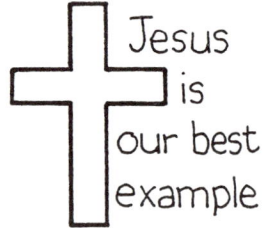

ISAIAH 30 vs 1-2

Jesus is our best example

LUKE 4 v1   JOHN 5 v19

✡ We can't make it without God!

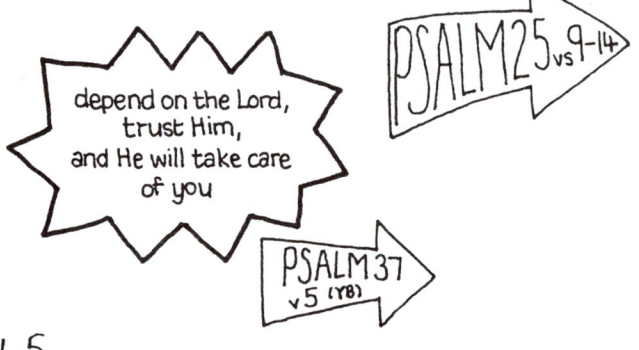

PSALM 25 vs 9-14

depend on the Lord, trust Him, and He will take care of you

PSALM 37 v5 (YB)

Mary said:

'I am the Lord's servant and I am willing to do whatever He wants'

LUKE 1 v38 (LB)

✡ God guides us in different ways:

✡ Through the Bible:

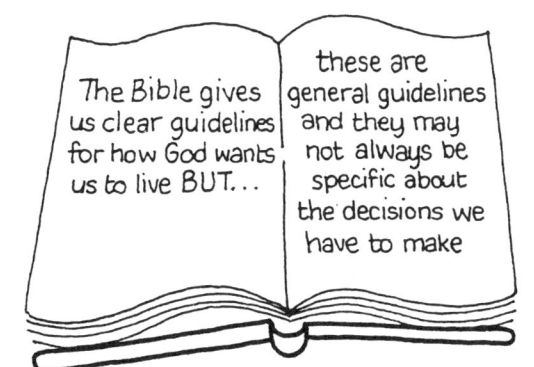

The Bible gives us clear guidelines for how God wants us to live BUT... these are general guidelines and they may not always be specific about the decisions we have to make

FAX — For example: Matthew 19 v 19 tells us 'love your neighbour as yourself' BUT... it doesn't tell us how when the baby's crying, the dog's barking and the music's on all night!

✡ When we are faced with major decisions we need to find out what God's particular will for us is

This doesn't mean opening the Bible and blindly sticking in a pin - hoping to find a relevant verse...

One of the best ways to know God's guidance is through regular Bible study

Often a verse will 'jump' off of the page and suddenly make sense in your situation

> 2 TIMOTHY 3 v 16

> PSALM 119 vs 105 + 130 - 133

☆ Through the Holy Spirit

like a friend's voice on the phone, the Holy Spirit helps us to recognize God's voice

JOHN 10 vs 3-4 ▷   ACTS 16 v 7 ▷

☆ God speaks as we pray

One of the ways that God speaks is by giving us a strong feeling of what He wants

ACTS 13 vs 1-3 ▷

1 JOHN 4 v 1 ▷

FAX — we need to LISTEN as we pray — not just talk!

is it loving? (1 John 4 v 16)

is it strengthening, encouraging and comforting? (1 Corinthians 14 v 3)

BUT we need to test our feelings:

☆ God might give us a strong desire to do something

PHILIPPIANS 2 v 13 ▷

☆ Sometimes He uses more unusual ways:

- PROPHECY (Acts 11 vs 27-28) (Acts 21 vs 10-11)
- VISIONS + PICTURES (Acts 16 v 10)
- DREAMS (Matt 1 v 20)
- ANGELS (Genesis 18) (Acts 12 v 7) (Matt 12 v 19)
- A VOICE (1 Sam. 3 vs 4-14)

✡ Through common sense

As Christians we can't just ignore common sense

PSALM 32 vs 8-9 →

2 TIMOTHY 2 v 7 →

FAX — 'God's promises of guidance were not given to save us the problem of thinking' (John Stott)

✡ Through advice from others

a wise man listens to advice

PROVERBS 15 v 22 →

PROVERBS 20 v 18 →

PROVERBS 12 v 15 →

It's good to get advice from other, maybe more experienced Christians — But be careful not to blame your advisers if things don't go quite how you'd have liked

✡ Through circumstances

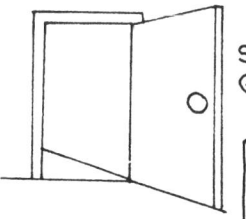

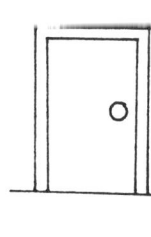

sometimes God opens doors

1 CORINTHIANS 16 v 9 →

sometimes God closes doors

ACTS 16 v 7 →

BUT Don't put too much emphasis on circumstances — sometimes we need to persevere despite them!

PROVERBS 16 v 9 →

GOD IS IN CONTROL!

don't rush things!

Sometimes we have to **WAIT**

→ HEBREWS 6 v 15

we all make mistakes

→ JOEL 2 v 25

but God **FORGIVES!**

Why and How should we tell others?

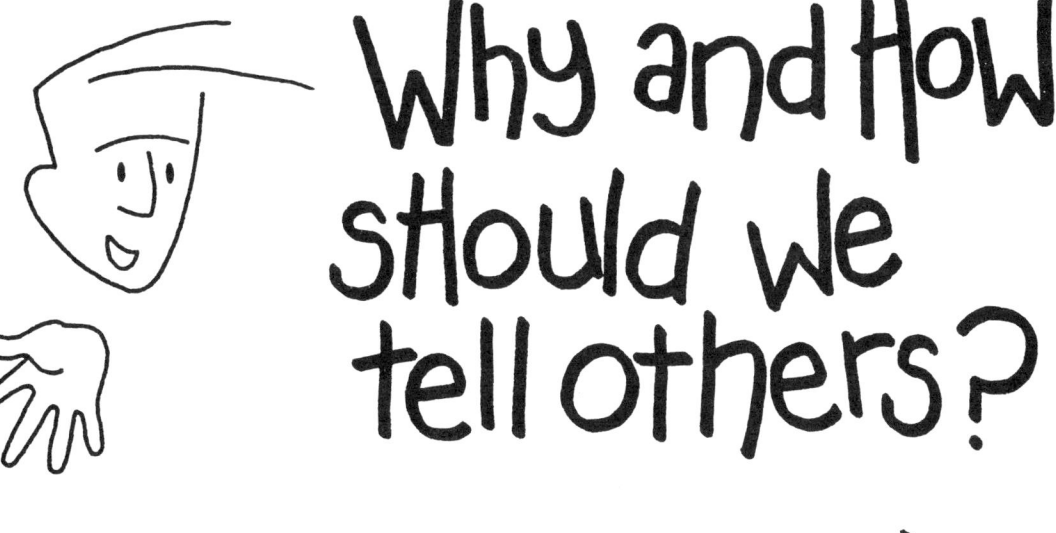

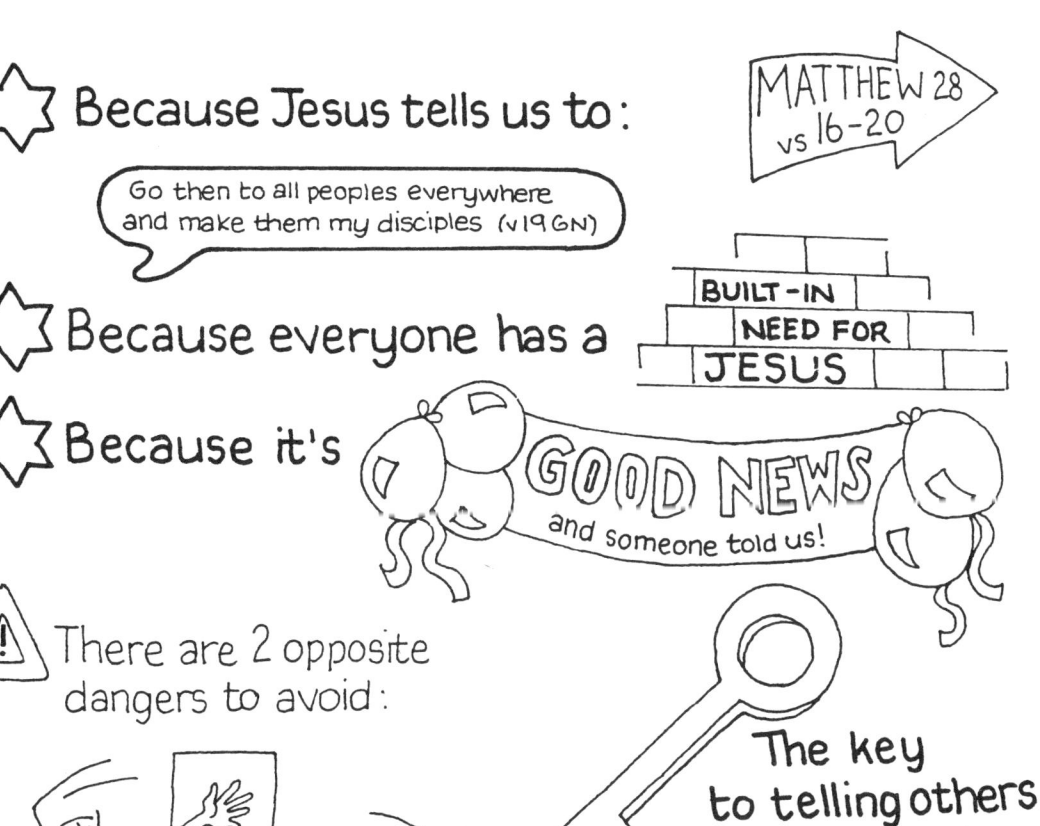

☆ Because Jesus tells us to:

MATTHEW 28 vs 16-20

"Go then to all peoples everywhere and make them my disciples (v19 GN)"

☆ Because everyone has a **BUILT-IN NEED FOR JESUS**

☆ Because it's **GOOD NEWS** and someone told us!

⚠ There are 2 opposite dangers to avoid:

insensitivity + fear

The key to telling others about Jesus is building relationships and trusting in God

50

✡ Presence

MATTHEW 5 vs 13-16

SALT

FAX: Salt was used to preserve meat and prevent decay. We are called to preserve God's standards in the world.

When people know we are Christians they watch how we live — our actions should match our words

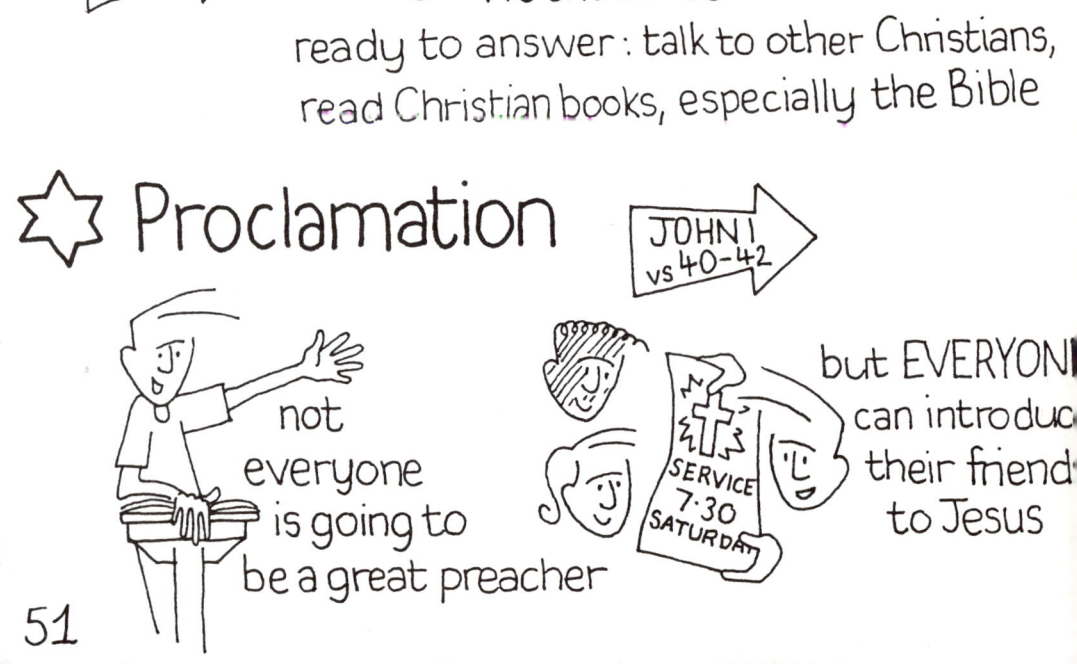

✡ Persuasion

2 CORINTHIANS 5 v 11

ACTS 17 vs 2-4

When we talk about what we believe, people will ask questions:

- what about other religions?
- if God loves us – why does he allow suffering?

We should be ready to answer: talk to other Christians, read Christian books, especially the Bible

✡ Proclamation

JOHN 1 vs 40-42

not everyone is going to be a great preacher

SERVICE 7:30 SATURDAY

but EVERYONE can introduce their friend to Jesus

☆ Power

ACTS 3

By God's Power even our most mixed-up messages can make an impact!

for the Good News we brought to you came not only with words, but with POWER

1 THESSALONIANS 1 v 5 (YB)

☆ Prayer

☆ to open blind eyes — **2 CORINTHIANS 4 v 4**

☆ for us to be bold — **ACTS 4 vs 29-31**

⟨SO⟩ Don't give up!

sometimes we don't know if what we've said has had any effect. We may find out later or we may not — **TRUST GOD!**

The Gospel... is the power God uses to save everyone who believes

ROMANS 1 v 16 (YB)

Does God Heal today?

BIBLE BASIS

☆ The Old Testament

☆ God's Promises — EXODUS 23 vs 25-26 — PSALM 41 v3

☆ God's Character — 'I am the Lord who heals you' — EXODUS 15 v26

☆ Examples of God's healing

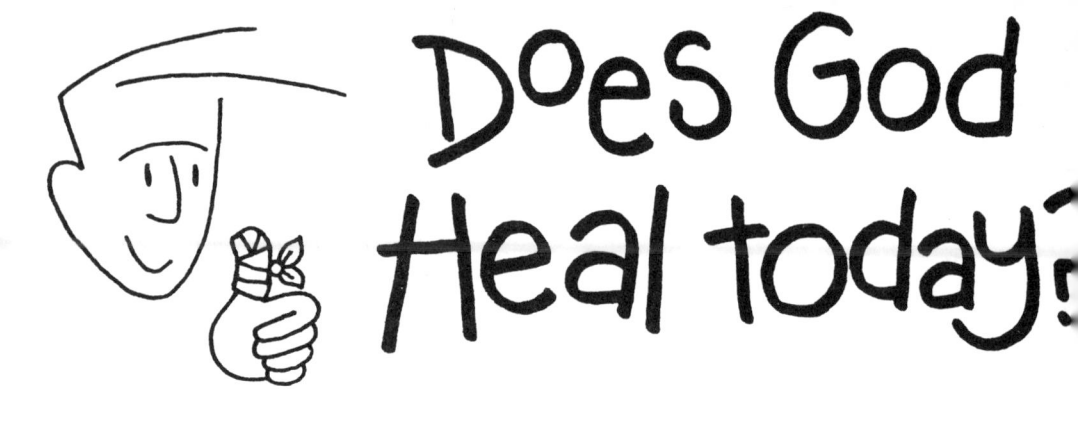

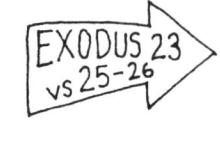

Naaman — 2 KINGS 5

Hezekiah — ISAIAH 38 + 39

It is in God's nature to heal us because He wants the VERY BEST FOR US!

53

✡ The example of Jesus

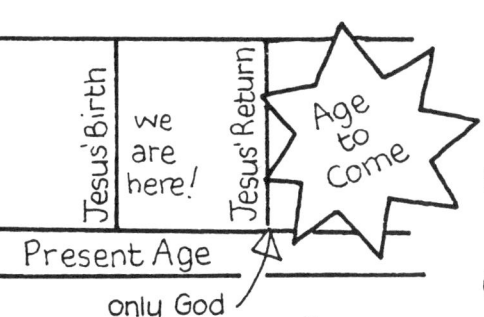

Diagram: Timeline showing "Jesus' Birth" → "we are here!" → "Jesus' Return" → "Age to Come". Labelled "Present Age". Note: "only God knows when this will be".

History can be divided into: the time up until Jesus' birth and the time since then in which we are living, history as we know it — and the time from when Jesus returns, which is yet to come.

When Jesus came the first time He was a weak and dependent baby, when He returns it will be with power and great glory' (Matthew 24 v 30)

For those who reject Jesus it will be a day of destruction (2 Thessalonians 1 vs 8-9)

For those who have accepted Him it will be time to receive their inheritance — it is the day all history is building up to. (Matthew 25 v 34)

In this new time we will have new bodies that will be 'glorious and imperishable' 1 Corinthians 15 vs 42-43). There will be no more crying or death or pain (Revelation 21 v 4). All who believe in Jesus will be totally healed on that day. When Jesus healed people and when God heals people today, it is a little piece of the age to come breaking into the present age.

✡ Jesus gave His disciples authority to heal and sent them out to do it.

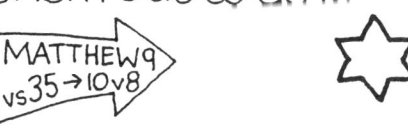

MATTHEW 9 vs 35 → 10 v 8

FAX — Over 25% of the Gospels tell us about JESUS HEALING

✡ Jesus sends 72 more to do the same

LUKE 10 vs 1-20

✡ Jesus sends US out too

'whoever believes in me will do what I do' (v12-GN)

JOHN 14 vs 9-14

MARK 16 vs 15-20

MATTHEW 28 vs 17-20

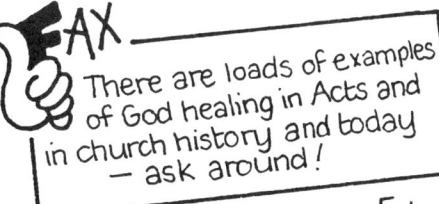

FAX — There are loads of examples of God healing in Acts and in church history and today — ask around!

☆ How do we pray for healing?

FAX: It is GOD WHO HEALS NOT US!

☆ Jesus healed people because He loved them. It's important that we love the people we pray for and respect their dignity.

→ MARK 1 v 41   → MATTHEW 9 v 36

☆ Our prayers don't need to be long and complicated. **SIMPLE IS BEST!**

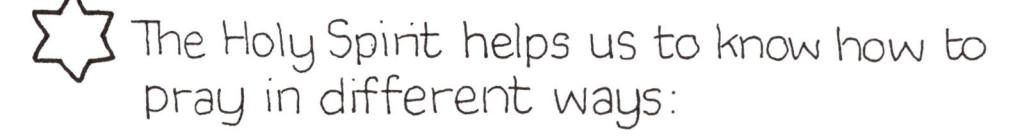

☆ The Holy Spirit helps us to know how to pray in different ways:

- ☆ we may get a **picture** in our minds
- ☆ or a **sympathy pain** in the same place someone is hurting
- ☆ it could be a **strong feeling**
- ☆ we may **hear or see words** in our minds
- ☆ or sometimes we **speak words** that the Spirit gives to us

☆ When we pray:

we should ask:
- where does it hurt?
- how long has it hurt?
- why do you think it hurts?

☆ Pray that God would heal in the name of Jesus

☆ Ask the Holy Spirit to fill the person

☆ Listen and be open to what God says

ALWAYS BE SENSITIVE TO HOW THE PERSON FEELS

☆ After praying, ask how they feel

☆ If the person has pain in a particular area it may be appropriate to put your hand there as you pray – BE SENSITIVE!

FAX — God heals in His timing don't be disappointed if that is not while you're there. Sometimes it is not until the person goes to be with God that they are healed.

PERSEVERE WITH FAITH!

MATTHEW 7 vs 7-8

What about the church?

⭐ The church is NOT:

SERVICES

Mornings 10·30
Evenings 6·30

CLERGY

Sermon Notes

ONE DENOMINATION

THE BUILDING

57

What is the church?

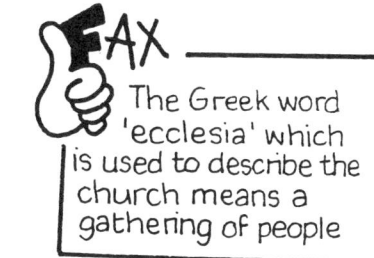

☆ The people of God

→ EPHESIANS 2 vs 19-22

FAX: The Greek word 'ecclesia' which is used to describe the church means a gathering of people

BAPTISM is a public symbol of Christianity

it signifies:

☆ That our old life is dead
→ I CORINTHIANS 6 v 11

☆ And a new life has begun
→ ROMANS 6 vs 3-5   → COLOSSIANS 2 v 12

☆ Through the Holy Spirit we become one of God's people: The church
→ I CORINTHIANS 12 v 13

☆ The universal church:

- The persecuted church
- The Third World
- The free world

→ EPHESIANS 3 vs 10 + 21
→ EPHESIANS 5 vs 23 + 25

FAX: There are 1,700 MILLION Christians in the world today

☆ Local churches:

Galatian churches → I CORINTHIANS 16 v 1

Asian churches → I CORINTHIANS 16 v 19

All churches → ROMANS 16 v 5   I CORINTHIANS 16 v 19

In the New Testament as today, the church met in large groups for celebration:

and in smaller groups to get to know each other, to minister to each other → EPHESIANS 4 v 2

and to use the gifts given by the Holy Spirit → I CORINTHIANS 12 vs 7-11

It's very important to have other Christians that you can meet with and trust.

The Family of God

☆ God as our Father → EPHESIANS 2 vs 14-18

☆ Jesus prayed: "...that they may be one" → JOHN 17 v 11

☆ 'make every effort to keep the unity of the Spirit' → EPHESIANS 4 v 3

☆ We're all brothers and sisters → 1 JOHN 4 v 19 - 5 v 1

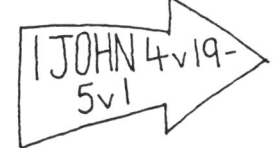

☆ Fellowship with God → 1 JOHN 1 v 3 → 2 CORINTHIANS 13 v 14

☆ And with one another → 1 JOHN 1 v 7 → HEBREWS 10 vs 24-25

✡ The Body of Christ

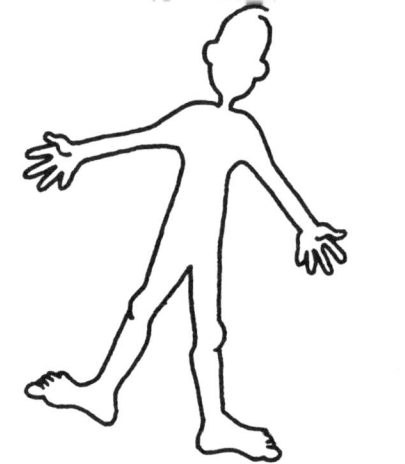

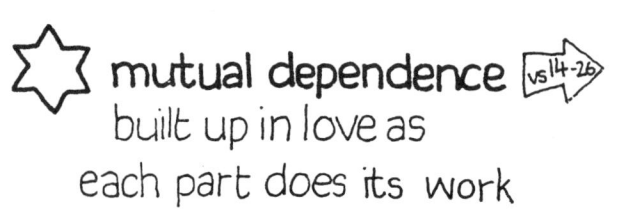

I CORINTHIANS 12 vs 1-26

✡ **unity** `vs 4-6`
the unity of the Spirit

✡ **diversity** `vs 7-11` `vs 28-30`
to each one of us
grace has been given

✡ **mutual dependence** `vs 14-26`
built up in love as
each part does its work

✡ A Holy Temple

EPHESIANS 2 vs 19-22

✡ built on a foundation of apostles and prophets (New Testament) v20

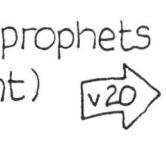

✡ Indwelt by God's Spirit v22

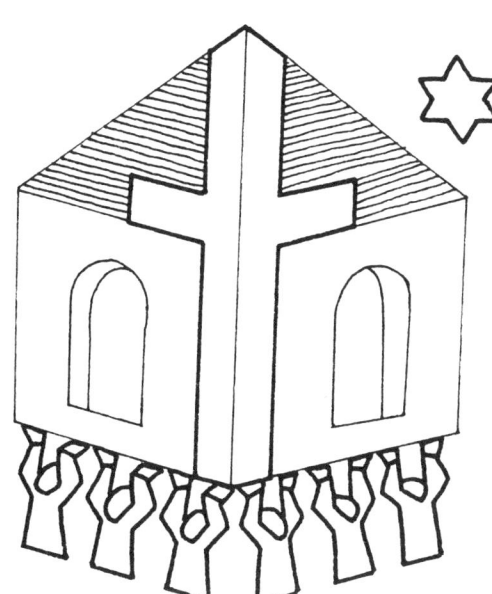

✡ Jesus as the cornerstone v20

✡ The Bride of Christ

EPHESIANS 5 vs 25-27

✡ Christ's (LOVE) for His church v25

How can I make the most of the rest of my life?

ROMANS 12

✡ **Do not conform**

'Do not conform any longer to the pattern of this world'

✡ Be transformed

'Let God transform you inwardly by a complete change'

`v2 NEB`

✡ Sincere love

Your love must be real. Hate what is evil, and hold on to what is GOOD!

`v9 YB`

✡ Enthusiasm for God

Serving the Lord with all your heart

`v11 YB`

✡ Good relationships

Do your best to live in peace with everyone

`v18 YB`

☆ 'Present your bodies...'

☆ as an **ACT OF WILL** 'offer your bodies'

- WHAT YOU HEAR
- WHAT YOU SEE
- WHAT YOU SAY
- LIVING SACRIFICE
- YOUR HANDS
- YOUR SEXUALITY
- YOUR MONEY
- YOUR AMBITION (Matthew 6 v 33)
- YOUR TIME
- YOU

It will involve sacrifice, it may involve suffering

☆ 'His good, pleasing and perfect will' v2→

God has a **GREAT PLAN** for our future

☆ 'In view of God's mercy...' v2→

NOTES

NOTES

NOTES